ALSO BY PHILIP LEVINE

POETRY

THE MERCY 1999

THEY FEED THEY LION AND THE NAMES OF THE LOST (REISSUE) 1999

UNSELECTED POEMS 1997

THE SIMPLE TRUTH 1994

WHAT WORK IS 1991

NEW SELECTED POEMS 1991

A WALK WITH TOM JEFFERSON 1988

SWEET WILL 1985

SELECTED POEMS 1984

ONE FOR THE ROSE 1981

7 YEARS FROM SOMEWHERE 1979

ASHES: POEMS NEW AND OLD 1979

THE NAMES OF THE LOST 1976

1933 1974

THEY FEED THEY LION 1972

RED DUST 1971

PILI'S WALL 1971

NOT THIS PIG 1968

ON THE EDGE 1963

ESSAYS

SO ASK 2003

THE BREAD OF TIME 1994

TRANSLATIONS

OFF THE MAP: SELECTED POEMS OF GLORIA FUERTES,
EDITED AND TRANSLATED WITH ADA LONG 1984

TARUMBA: THE SELECTED POEMS OF JAIME SABINES,
EDITED AND TRANSLATED WITH ERNESTO TREJO 1979

INTERVIEWS

DON'T ASK 1981

BREATH

BREATH

Poems by

PHILIP LEVINE

Alfred A. Knopf   *New York 2004*

THIS IS A BORZOI BOOK
PUBLISHED BY ALFRED A. KNOPF

Copyright © 2004 by Philip Levine

All rights reserved under International and Pan-American Copyright
Conventions. Published in the United States by Alfred A. Knopf,
a division of Random House, Inc., New York, and simultaneously
in Canada by Random House of Canada Limited, Toronto.
Distributed by Random House, Inc., New York.

www.randomhouse.com/knopf/poetry

Knopf, Borzoi Books, and the colophon are registered
trademarks of Random House, Inc.

My thanks to the editors of the following publications
in which these poems first appeared:
ATLANTIC MONTHLY: "The Lesson"
BLACKBIRD: "Breakfasts with Joachim"
DOUBLETAKE: "The Esquire" & "The Invention of the Fado"
FIELD: "My Given Name"
FIRST OF THE MONTH: "On 52nd Street"
FIVE POINTS: "Praise," "My Brother, Antonio, the Baker,"
& "On a Photograph of Simon Karaday"
GEORGIA REVIEW: "Dust," "Naming," & "The Genius"
IMAGE: "When the Shift Was Over"
KENYON REVIEW: "My Father in the Wind"
NEW YORKER: "Gospel," "The Two," "A View of Home,"
"Home for the Holidays," "For a *Duro*," & "Yenkl"
POETRY: "Storms," "Keats in California,"
"1/1/2000," & "Call It Music"
SLATE: "The West Wind"
SOUTHERN REVIEW: "Houses in Order"
THIRD COAST: "Dutch Treat"
YALE REVIEW: "The Great Truth," "Moradian," &
"Today and Two Thousand Years from Now"

Library of Congress Cataloging-in-Publication Data
Levine, Philip [date]
Breath : poems / by Philip Levine.— 1st ed.
p. cm.
ISBN 1-4000-4291-7
I. Title.
PS3562.E9B73 2004
811'.54—dc22   2004040839

Manufactured in the United States of America

FIRST EDITION

IN MEMORY OF WILLIAM MAXWELL &
WILLIAM MATTHEWS

"They put a skin on everything they said."

Some days I catch a rhythm, almost a song
in my own breath.

CONTENTS

Contents

I

GOSPEL

The new grass rising in the hills,
the cows loitering in the morning chill,
a dozen or more old browns hidden
in the shadows of the cottonwoods
beside the streambed. I go higher
to where the road gives up and there's
only a faint path strewn with lupine
between the mountain oaks. I don't
ask myself what I'm looking for.
I didn't come for answers
to a place like this, I came to walk
on the earth, still cold, still silent.
Still ungiving, I've said to myself,
although it greets me with last year's
dead thistles and this year's
hard spines, early-blooming
wild onions, the curling remains
of spider's cloth. What did I bring
to the dance? In my back pocket
a crushed letter from a woman
I've never met bearing bad news
I can do nothing about. So I wander
these woods half sightless while
a west wind picks up in the trees
clustered above. The pines make
a music like no other, rising and
falling like a distant surf at night
that calms the darkness before
first light. "Soughing" we call it, from
Old English, no less. How weightless
words are when nothing will do.

PRAISE

July. Central California. The heat comes on
and on and on until I think I can't bear
even another day of it, but of course I can.

Dust rises and falls on the dry paths, the air
is a dense yellow one moment, and then the wind
swirls the dark columns of dirt away and lifts

the lower boughs of the alder. When I close
my eyes I can hear a music, perhaps tunes
recalled from long-gone summers in Detroit.

I begin to sing, and my cracked voice goes out
over the bowed heads of onions and the rising ones
of the giant sunflowers whose seeds arrived

last autumn from Amsterdam, sent by a friend
now dead. I see a bird, a wren I think,
a quick and delicate gray creature who darts

into a plum tree and turns her back on me
to swell out her feathers. When we both freeze
the music comes back so softly at first I hear

only the muted conversations of dry dull sheaves,
the breath released from runners of squash,
the breath taken back, and then the old themes

restated until the garden is dense with song.
"Lejan Kwint," I hum the name of my lost friend
who clung to his life until he could not cling.

The great heads of the sunflowers fall and rise
in the winds they make. The bird dares the noon light
to pick from bloom to bloom, and now I see

the tiny puffed-out breast is smeared with rose.
A finch, I think, a finch for Lejan Kwint,
whose seeds beget more seeds through the long days

until the brutal air itself groans with his praise.

STORMS

After the storm of his dying,
after the phone calls and letters
stopped, after the sudden outbursts
of tears, seizures that came on me
without warning and left me ashamed,
after those passed, he entered my dreams
one June morning, young and slender
again, in leather jacket and jeans.
Yes, of course he was dead! He waved
it away, smiling. It was nothing
to worry about, it was just life,
he said, laughing now at the joke.
Restless, he paced the room, raising
his arms in a gesture of disgust
or surrender, and shook his head
back and forth. We were in a place
I didn't know, a second-floor
apartment somewhere in Brooklyn
or Detroit. A row of poplars
lashed with rain was keening, wind
bowed, outside the high rear windows
before which like a dancer he
slowly sank to the bare wood floor,
head downcast. All my life I've been
waiting for them, those I needed,
to come back, and now I could feel
him slipping away. I could hear
the day breaking in on our lives
just as he placed one hand in mine
and looked up, his dark eyes open
wide, accepting. Yes, it had stormed.
When I rose to open the shutters
the street was black with rain, the sky

above the trees a perfect blue,
the city still. All day I searched
shopwindows, record bins, bookstores,
even a Greek bakery for a hint
of what I can't say. Late afternoon
I gave up and crossed the great bridge
toward home, the traffic groaning
below me. Ahead the city spread
out, my neighborhood thick with trees,
below them wharves and warehouses
solid and brooding. And above
the same sky, blue, expressionless
as always, without the least sign
of the arched rainbow of his faith.

THE GREAT TRUTH

Early Sunday morning he'd drive the black Packard
to the "island"—as he called it—a public park
in the Detroit River, and walk slowly
along the horse paths, both hands clasped
together behind his back. He always wore the good gray suit,
white shirt stiffly starched, black polished wing tips.
Why the horse paths, I wondered, that led us away
from the river, the broad view of the skyline,
the ore boats headed toward unknown, exotic ports,
why into the silent darkened woods, fringed
with nettled scrub and echoing with crow calls.
The September he came back from prison, penniless,
and took a murderous night job in the forge room
at Cadillac, he'd rise before dawn to waken me
in the still house. Whatever he was looking for
he never said, and I was too young to ask.
Eleven then, a growing boy, I believed
there were answers. I believed one morning
he'd turn suddenly to tell me why men and boys
went into such forbidding places or pacing
beside him, I would see some transformation
up ahead where the sky, faceless and gray, hung
above the pin oaks, and know for once the world
was not the world, that the breath battering
my ears and catching in my chest was more
than only my breath. I'd know all this was
something else, something unnamable
that included me.

              That first Sunday no one entered
my room in the December dark to touch me
on the shoulder, I slept till almost noon.
The Packard gone, I thought, and Uncle Nate—

as I'd taken to calling him—gone as well.
I found him in shirtsleeves shoveling last night's snow
off the front steps and singing hillbilly songs.
The house is still there, one of those ghost houses
from another era with mock turrets and steep eaves
the tourists photograph. It sits on a block
of rubble and nothing waiting for JFK
to come back from Dallas and declare a new
New Frontier. The last time I saw Uncle Nate
was seventeen years ago in a bar on Linwood
with a woman anxious to leave. I had to
tell him who I was, "Phil from the old house
on Riopelle." He put his head down on the bar,
closed his eyes, and said, "Oh my God, oh my God,"
and nothing more. Yesterday morning my brother
drove me out to the island. It was raining
and he waited with coffee and the *Free Press*
in the echoing rotunda while I walked
the old trails, rutted now by tire tracks, the ground
spongy and alive in April. I felt foolish
under a huge black umbrella, but no one else
was out to see me, so I went on into a stand
of new spruce and hemlock gleaming in the rain
that drummed softly into last year's dead needles.
Up ahead what little I could see of sky
lightened as though urging me toward something
waiting for me more than half a century, some
great truth to live by now that it was too late
to live in the world other than I do.

ON 52ND STREET

Down sat Bud, raised his hands,
the Deuces silenced, the lights
lowered, and breath gathered
for the coming storm. Then nothing,
not a single note. Outside starlight
from heaven fell unseen, a quarter-
moon, promised, was no show,
ditto the rain. Late August of '50,
NYC, the long summer of abundance
and our new war. In the mirror behind
the bar, the spirits—imitating us—
stared at themselves. At the bar
the tenor player up from Philly shut
his eyes and whispered to no one,
"Same thing last night." Everyone
been coming all week long
to hear *this*. The big brown bass
sighed and slumped against
the piano, the cymbals held
their dry cheeks and stopped
chicking and chucking. We went
back to drinking and ignored
the unignorable. When the door
swung open, it was Pettiford
in work clothes, midnight suit,
starched shirt, narrow black tie,
spit-shined shoes, as ready
as he'd ever be. Eyebrows
raised, the Irish bartender
shook his head, so Pettiford eased
himself down at an empty table,
closed up his *Herald Tribune*,
and shook his head. Did the TV

come on, did the jukebox bring us
Dinah Washington, did the stars
keep their appointments, did the moon
show, quartered or full, sprinkling
its soft light down? The night's
still there, just where it was, just
where it'll always be without
its music. You're still there too,
holding your breath. Bud walked out.

MORADIAN

He is not an apparition. After midnight,
coming home from the job at Chevy,
he materializes out of the darkness.
Yes, I'm weary, but I'm also sober,
and I know he's beside me matching
me stride for stride. I wait for words
which never come. Some men don't
live by words no matter how much
they know, and he knows it all. Dressed
in the same dark pin-striped suit
he wore to our engineering class years
before, wearing also that downward cast
of his eyes, the slight flush of blood along
the shaved cheekbones. Never did we
call him Johnny; even at sixteen
he was John, a man waiting to enter
a man's world, the one that would kill him.
Had he seen me when I was young?
He sat stoically at his desk beside me
staring off into nothing or perhaps
the future while quaint Mr. Kostick,
our drawing teacher, went from student
to student to mark our progress, always
avoiding John. After the Christmas break
of '43 his desk sat empty and the word
was the Marine Corps or the paratroopers
on some secret Pacific venture. No one
really knew until his name appeared
in a long list in the *Free Press*. Where were
the Marianas? I had to take the big atlas
down from the shelf, sit it in my lap,
sweating, and pore over that expanse
to find the small white dots swimming

in a great sea of deep blue, while outside
our little study window the October night
came on one light after another
in the street's closed houses. Somewhere
there must be a yellowing photograph
of a black-haired boy in shorts, shy, smiling,
already looking away, there must be
a pile of letters to someone, useless words
that said what every boy has to say or,
if they're gone, a sister who recalls
his early needs, those breathless cries
each of us stifles. He can't just be me,
smaller now than I, his damp hands empty,
his breath my breath, his silence also mine
in the face of our life, he just can't be.

THE WEST WIND

When the winter wind
moves through the ash trees
in my yard I hear
the past years calling
in the pale voices
of the air. The words,
caught in the branches,
echo a moment
before they fade out.
The wind calms, the trees
go back to being
merely trees and not
seven messengers
from another world,
if that's what they were.
The alder, older,
harbors a few leaves
from last fall, black, curled,
a silent chorus
for all those we've left
behind. Suddenly
at my back I feel
a new wind come on,
chilling, relentless,
with all the power
of loss, the meaning
unmistakable.

KEATS IN CALIFORNIA

The wisteria has come and gone, the plum trees
have burned like candles in the cup of earth,
the almond has shed its pure blossoms
in a soft ring around the trunk. Iris,
rose, tulip, hillsides of poppy and lupine,
gorse, wild mustard, California is blazing
in the foolish winds of April. I have been
reading Keats—the poems, the letters, the life—
for the first time in my 70th year, and I
have been watching television after dinner
as though it could bring me some obscure,
distant sign of hope. This morning I rose
late to the soft light off the eucalyptus
and the overbearing odor of orange blossoms.
The trees will give another year. They are giving.
The few, petty clouds will blow away
before noon, and we will have sunshine
without fault, china-blue skies, and the bees
gathering to splatter their little honey dots
on my windshield. If I drive to the foothills
I can see fields of wildflowers on fire until
I have to look away from so much life.
I could ask myself, Have I made a Soul
today, have I sucked at the teat of the Heart
flooded with the experience of a world like ours?
Have I become a man one more time? At twenty
it made sense. I put down *The Collected Poems,*
left the reserve room of the Wayne library
to wander the streets of Detroit under a gray
soiled sky. It was spring there too, and the bells
rang at noon. The outpatients from Harper
waited timidly under the great stone cross
of the Presbyterian church for the trolley

on Woodward Avenue, their pinched faces flushed
with terror. The black tower tilted in the wind
as though it too were coming down. It made sense.
Before dark I'll feel the lassitude enter
first my arms and legs and spread like water
toward the deep organs. I'll lie on my bed
hearing the quail bark as they scurry
from cover to cover in their restless searching
after sustenance. This place can break your heart.

TODAY AND TWO THOUSAND
YEARS FROM NOW

The job is over. We stand under the trees
waiting to be told what to do,
but the job is over.

The darkness pours between the branches above,
but the moon's not yet
on its walk

through the night sky trailed by stars.
Suddenly a match flares, I see
there are only us two,

you and me, alone together in the great room
of the night world, two laborers
with nothing to do,

so I lean to the little flame and light my Lucky
and thank you, comrade, and again
we are in the dark.

Let me now predict the future. Two thousand years
from now we two will be older,
wiser, having escaped

the fleeting incarnations of workingmen.
We will have risen from the earth
of southern Michigan

through the tangled roots of Chinese elms
or ancient rosebushes to take
the tainted air

into our leaves and send it back, purified,
down the same trail we took
to escape the dark.

Two thousand years passed in a flash to shed
no more light than a wooden match
gave under the trees

when you and I were lost kids, more scared than
now, but warm, useless, with names
and different faces.

THE TWO

When he gets off work at Packard, they meet
outside a diner on Grand Boulevard. He's tired,
a bit depressed, and smelling the exhaustion
on his own breath, he kisses her carefully
on her left cheek. Early April, and the weather
has not decided if this is spring, winter, or what.
The two gaze upward at the sky, which gives
nothing away: the low clouds break here and there
and let in tiny slices of a pure blue heaven.
The day is like us, she thinks; it hasn't decided
what to become. The traffic light at Linwood
goes from red to green and the trucks start up,
so that when he says, "Would you like to eat?"
she hears a jumble of words that means nothing,
though spiced with things she cannot believe,
"wooden Jew" and "lucky meat." He's been up
late, she thinks, he's tired of the job, perhaps tired
of their morning meetings, but then he bows
from the waist and holds the door open
for her to enter the diner, and the thick
odor of bacon frying and new potatoes
greets them both, and taking heart she enters
to peer through the thick cloud of tobacco smoke
to see if "their booth" is available.
F. Scott Fitzgerald wrote that there were no
second acts in America, but he knew neither
this man nor this woman and no one else
like them unless he stayed late at the office
to test his famous one-liner, "We keep you clean
in Muscatine," on the woman emptying
his wastebasket. Fitzgerald never wrote
with someone present, except for this woman
in a gray uniform whose comings and goings

went unnoticed even on those December evenings
she worked late while the snow fell silently
on the windowsills and the new fluorescent lights
blinked on and off. Get back to the two, you say.
Not who ordered poached eggs, who ordered
only toast and coffee, who shared the bacon
with the other, but what became of the two
when this poem ended, whose arms held whom,
who first said "I love you" and truly meant it,
and who misunderstood the words, so longed
for and yet still so unexpected, and began
suddenly to scream and curse until the waitress
asked them both to leave. The Packard plant closed
years before I left Detroit, the diner was burned
to the ground in '67, two years before my oldest son
fled to Sweden to escape the American dream.
"And the lovers?" you ask. I wrote nothing about lovers.
Take a look. Clouds, trucks, traffic lights, a diner, work,
a wooden shoe, East Moline, poached eggs, the perfume
of frying bacon, the chaos of language, the spices
of spent breath after eight hours of night work.
Can you hear all I feared and never dared to write?
Why the two are more real than either you or me,
why I never returned to keep them in my life,
how little I now mean to myself or anyone else,
what any of this could mean, where you found
the patience to endure these truths and confusions?

II

MY BROTHER, ANTONIO, THE BAKER

Did the wind blow that night? When did it not?
I'd ask you if you hadn't gone underground
lugging the answer with you.
Twenty-eight years old, on our way home
after a twelve-hour shift baking Wonder bread
for the sleeping prisoners in the drunk tank
at the Canfield Station dreaming of a breakfast
of horse cock and mattress stuffing.
(Oh, the luxuries of 1955! How fully we lived—
the working classes and the law-abiding dregs—
on buttered toast and grilled-cheese sandwiches
as the nation braced itself for pâté and pasta.)
To myself I smelled like a new mother minus
the aura of talcum and the airborne acrid aromas
of cotton diapers. Today I'd be labeled
nurturing and bountiful instead
of vegetal and weird. A blurred moon was out,
we both saw it; I know because, leaning back,
eyes closed on a ruined sky, you did your thing,
welcoming the "bright orb" waning in the west,
"Moon that rained down its silver coins
on the darkened Duero and the sleeping fields
of Soria." Did I look like you, my face
anonymous and pure, bleached with flour,
my eyes glistening with the power of neon light
or self-love? Two grown men, side by side,
one babbling joyfully to the universe
that couldn't care less, while the other
practiced for middle age. A single crow settled
on the boiler above the Chinese restaurant,
his feathers riffling, and I took it for a sign.
A second sign was the couple exiting
the all-night pharmacy; the man came first

through the glass door, a small white sack in hand,
and let the door swing shut. Then she appeared,
one hand covering her eyes to keep
the moonlight at bay. They stood not talking
while he looked first left, then right, then left
again as flakes of darkness sifted upward
toward the streetlight. The place began to rumble
as though this were the end. You spoke again,
only this time you described someone humble
walking alone in darkness. I could see
the streetcar turning off Joy Road,
swaying down the tracks toward us,
its windows on fire. There must have been a wind,
a west wind. What else could have blown
the aura of forsythia through the town
and materialized one crosstown streetcar
never before on time? A spring wind
freighted with hope. I remember
thinking that at last you might shut up.
An old woman stood to give you
her seat as though you were angelic
or pregnant. When her eyes spilled over
with happiness, I saw she took your words
to heart as I never could. Maybe she recalled
the Duero, the fields asleep in moonlight,
maybe the words were music to her,
original and whole, words that took her home
to Soria or Kraków or wherever,
maybe she was not an old woman at all
but an oracle in drag who saw you as you were
and saw, too, you couldn't last the night.

OUR REDS

Let us bless the three wild Reds
of our school days. Bless how easily
gaunt Vallejo would lose control,
the blood rushing to his depleted face
while his mistress in a torn trench coat
stroked his padded shoulders to calm him.
We'll call him Vallejo after the poet
only because he vaulted into speech
in such a headlong rush. (In truth
his name was Slovakian.) We'll call
her Lupino after the film star
because she was more beautiful
in memory than in fact, her cheeks
drawn over fine bones, her hair
tumbling down from under the beret,
hair we loved and called "dirty blond."
Vallejo would rise in class, unasked,
to interrupt "the tired fascist swill"
the stunned professor was giving out:
"The proper function of a teacher
is to inform the unformed cadres
of the exploited classes regarding
the nature of their enslavement
to an estate sold to the masters
of the means of production." Lupino
would rise quietly beside him to show
solidarity and to begin
her therapy. Two-ton Cohen would
join in flashing his party cards
for all to see and invoking
the sacred triads of Hegel. And we,
the unformed and uninformed, dropped
our pencils and groaned with gladness

to be quit of Aristotle's *Ethics,*
or the monetary theories
of James K. Polk, and stared into
a future of rotund potential
fulfilled. They are gone now, the three
—Vallejo, Lupino, Cohen—
into an America no one wanted
or something even worse, so bless
their certainties, their fiery voices
we so easily resisted, their tired eyes,
their cheeks flushed with sudden blood,
bless their rhetoric, bless their zeal,
bless their costumes and their cards,
bless their faith in us, especially
that faith, that hideous innocence.

A VIEW OF HOME

From Ontario's shore one sees
the smoking stacks of breweries,
the ore boats beached and fuming,
the satanic stove factory
where my great-uncle lost faith
in serf work, and sold his birthright,
his hip boots, his gauntlets
of cracked leather, his gold watch.
"Bye! Bye!" he sang from the window
of the train, his face aglow
with the joy of the adventure.
He was going back to die for good
Czar Nicholas. The waters of life
are pure, the Tao says, but our river
is salted with blown truck tires,
nonunion organizers, dead carp
floating silver side up, and is pulled
by a tide of money, and whatever it
nourishes turns to pure shit.

THE LESSON

Early in the final industrial century
on the street where I was born lived
a doctor who smoked black shag
and walked his dog each morning
as he muttered to himself in a language
only the dog knew. The doctor had saved
my brother's life, the story went, reached
two stained fingers down his throat
to extract a chicken bone and then
bowed to kiss the ring-encrusted hand
of my beautiful mother, a young widow
on the lookout for a professional.
Years before, before the invention of smog,
before Fluid Drive, the eight-hour day,
the iron lung, I'd come into the world
in a shower of industrial filth raining
from the bruised sky above Detroit.
Time did not stop. Mother married
a bland wizard in clutch plates
and drive shafts. My uncles went off
to their world wars, and I began a career
in root vegetables. Each morning,
just as the dark expired, the corner church
tolled its bells. Beyond the church
an oily river ran both day and night
and there along its banks I first conversed
with the doctor and Waldo, his dog.
"Young man," he said in words
resembling English, "you would dress
heavy for autumn, scarf, hat, gloves.
Not to smoke," he added, "as I do."
Eleven, small for my age but ambitious,
I took whatever good advice I got,

though I knew then what I know
now: the past, not the future, was mine.
If I told you he and I became pals
even though I barely understood him,
would you doubt me? Wakened before dawn
by the Catholic bells, I would dress
in the dark—remembering scarf, hat, gloves—
to make my way into the deserted streets
to where Waldo and his master ambled
the riverbank. Sixty-four years ago,
and each morning is frozen in memory,
each a lesson in what was to come.
What was to come? you ask. This world
as we have it, utterly unknowable,
utterly unacceptable, utterly unlovable,
the world we waken to each day
with or without bells. The lesson was
in his hands, one holding a cigarette,
the other buried in blond dog fur, and in
his words thick with laughter, hushed,
incomprehensible, words that were sound
only without sense, just as these must be.
Staring into the moist eyes of my maestro,
I heard the lost voices of creation running
over stones as the last darkness sifted upward,
voices saddened by the milky residue
of machine shops and spangled with first light,
discordant, harsh, but voices nonetheless.

DUTCH TREAT

A railroad station in a suburb of Amsterdam,
early June, the present. An amplified voice begins
suddenly to address me, for I am who is here,

to speak in a garbled stream of vowels and gutturals
for the pure pleasure of the woman who is speaking
without the least meaning or concern for meaning.

A woman I can't see, under forty years of age,
over two hundred pounds, and trained to sing Wagner,
a woman with two growing children and no husband,

unmarried just the once but no longer bitter
about the whole affair. In their better moments
the Dutch are a rational people. They learn to make do

with very little space and have learned also to keep
an intelligent distance even when herded together
or face-to-face no more than a foot apart.

They have learned, perhaps from their many travels,
to substitute small, odd household pets, cats—
which they call *pookies*—toy dogs, birds,

fish, stunned rodents, for children and parents,
for even the promised one who might sail serenely
into their lives laden with understanding and soul,

vowing to remain forever. They manage to live
below sea level and eat raw herring during three months—
April, May, and June—in times of peace and survive,

so when they speak directly to me, as now, I listen.
I forget to march to a different drummer, I forget
to march at all. Instead I stand at attention,

my hands clasped behind me, my hat straight, my ears
open to the storm of ruined original music pouring
around me like California champagne and lap it up.

THE ESQUIRE

The Esquire was part bowling alley, part
nightclub, so when the musicians played
we sat at our tables wondering how
they could go on over the crashing pins,
the men shouting and cursing, the women's
laughter high and false. Bernie, Tassone,
Williams, and I nursed our drinks, saying
as little as possible while the bass player,
a young Italian kid, Tassone's cousin,
raised his dark sweat-streaked face heavenward
and hummed as he bowed, his eyes closed up
as though he'd entered another life.
"The Man I Love," the balding drummer
whispered into the mike, and a woman,
brown-skinned, no less than forty, appeared
from nowhere and began to sing in a voice
roughened by smoke, a voice barely there.
"She could be my sister," Bernie said.
Blond, pale, Slavic, the favorite son,
he told us, of a Polish nobleman, though his mother
worked nights at Ford Rouge. The singer
held out her long, bare, muscular arms
as though offering the world
more than it ever gave, and she too turned
her face upward, eyes closed, to address
someone not there. In seven hours it would be
Monday morning, a yellow sun would rise
over the great snowy wastes of the parking lots.
I turned and Bernie was crying without sound,
the tears streaming down his long, angular face
shamelessly. "I want to be held," he said,
"just once I want to be held as a man."
And you ask what happened later, did

Bernie wait until the place closed down
to offer the singer a ride home, did I
loan him my car, a black four-door Kaiser
on its last legs, did Tassone's cousin,
severe in his long black overcoat, die
that night from a heroin overdose or was it
on another night behind another club,
did Williams go off to Korea
in Truman's army as he said he would,
did I refuse and wind up in my own hell?
None of that matters now. The sun rose on time
over the great parking lots, empty now
that we're all too old or too dead to work.

HOME FOR THE HOLIDAYS

Does anyone give a shit? Not
I, said the little brown mouse.
And so to bed, said Mother,
but no one was listening.
Praise the Lord, said the radio,
the radio said Praise the Lord
again, and the television
turned its back on the room.

Turnips for wisdom, eggplant
for beauty, parsnips for ease,
cabbage for size, a raw egg
for the hair, a slice of ham
to seize the hips, for the nose
foxglove and salt, for grace
ice-cold water poured from
way high up to way down low.

Everyone sits at the big table
in the dark. The empty plates
moon, the silverware stars,
the napkins scrub their hands.
I'm home, says the front door.
The windows are deep in thought,
the roof has taken off its hat.
Nothing to do, chants the toilet.

BREAKFASTS WITH JOACHIM

Sunday morning at Mel's Country Kitchen,
the place quiet, the locals bowing
to their heaped plates, Joachim let go with
"The Jews done it!" A dozen forks clattered,
the place grew eerie, and then he added
in fake Okie, "Moses went up that hill
to bring back God's word for us here."
Everyone went back to stuffing their faces;
Joachim nibbled on dry toast and sipped
his unsweetened tea. Why he wanted people
to think he was a gun-toting redneck
I never knew. Except for his time in Spain
I doubt he'd fired a gun. He wouldn't talk
about those years except to say, only once,
"I was just a kid looking for adventure."
I found his name in an obscure history
of the Lincoln Brigade; "Joachim Barron,
missing in action, Teruel, 1937,"
a notation he refused to clarify.
After breakfast we drove to the river
to exercise his little gray mongrel, Ginsberg,
who adored him. "Howl!" he commanded.
The mutt raised his muzzle and let go
with a long, mournful wail. I confess
I adored him too, especially then, walking
the riverbank overgrown with burdocks,
milkweed, thistles in early October.
Joachim in his blue suit and cordovans
bowing to inspect whatever dried blooms
he found and to confer their Latin
designations. "Gold!" he once shouted, holding
out a stone as Ginsberg danced around him.
"Really?" I said. "No, beautiful, worthless mica."

With spit he brought the grays and browns
swimming to the surface. The true gold
was Joachim, dressed like a viceroy except
for a tired black and red scarf brought back
from Spain, stained with the earth of Catalunya,
"What they buried the good Machado in
in '39." His perfect shoes sinking
in mud, he recited the opening stanzas
of "The Crime Was in Granada" in Spanish
and added, "The only bad poem he wrote."
Even when he was most alive I doubt
he knew he embodied what he worshipped,
the exquisite in the commonplace, or that
he dreamed the daily world could turn
that fast and all he treasured turn to dust
or nothing and leave me hunting
everywhere for what I'd never find
in all the years to come, salt for the spirit.

FOR A *DURO*

For a *duro* you got a night out of the wind.
(A *duro* was a five-peseta coin bearing
Franco's profile, the hooked nose tipped
upward as though he alone received
the breath of God. Back in '65
only he did receive the breath of God.)
For a *duro* you could lie down in the hallway
of the Hotel Splendide in your Sunday suit,
sleep under the lights, and rise in time
to bless the Son's first coming. For a *duro*
you could have a coffee and a plain roll
that would shatter like glass. For a *duro*
you could have it all, the cars, the women,
the seven-course meal and a sea view,
with the waitress bending to your cheek
to ask reverently, "More butter?" For a *duro*
I bought a pack of Antillanas and gave one
to the only traveler in the deserted terminal,
a soldier in uniform. When he bowed
to receive a light I saw the milky nape,
unlined. He must still be there, waiting.
The hotel is gone, the building remains,
a pet hospital and animal refectory
overseen by Señor Esteban Ganz arrayed
for work this morning in white coat,
dark tie, and soiled sneakers. Modestly
he shows me three lobo pups, pintos,
saved from slaughter, the striped feral cats
pacing the big cage like tigers, the toucan
leveled by an unknown virus but now
alert and preening. Riotous colors:
reds, greens, and illuminated golds
suitable for banners proclaiming inter-
galactic peace the moment it arrives.   *37*

HOUSES IN ORDER

In cardboard boxes under the Williamsburg Bridge
a congregation of mature rats founds a new order
based on the oldest religious principle: they eat
whatever they can get their teeth into. By day
they move slowly about their kingdom, some days
so slowly they seem for hours on end to become
holy relics or the stained brown backgrounds
to events foretold in parables to do with
the savor of salt, the mysteries of mustard seeds,
meat, bones, loaves, and fishes. When you look
back they've gone into water or air, they've joined
the falling rain that makes vision so difficult
even for the visionary. The little houses keep
their secrets the way windowless houses always do,
though their walls and roofs proclaim the hour's
holy names—Nike and Converse, Panasonic and Walk-
man—and though they let light leak in through
their teeth-torn ports and darkness out from under
their lids, they're closed to all but the eyes
of the faithful. These dull pilgrims contemplate
the business of gathering and hunting while the day
hangs on and the traffic drones on the bridge above.
Soon the headlights come on, singly or in pairs,
the rain gleams through the taut cables,
no moon rises above the island where now they are
among us, each one doing a morsel of God's work
until their small jaws ache from so much prayer.

DUST

I

My wife tells me that when she was six
she came home from school to an empty house,
put down her lunch box, sat on a hassock
by her father's chair, and simply waited.
Someone known would return home soon, she was sure.
The house was still, silent, holding its breath,
the late-afternoon sunlight streamed in
the unshaded windows and turned the dust
into tiny golden planets floating
before her. Sixty-four years later
she declares, "It was beautiful," and goes
on to describe the sense of awe and peace
before this vision of the universe
that descended from nowhere or perhaps
rose from within. North-central Iowa,
1933, her grandmother's house.
Nothing else remains of the day. She gazes
into space seeing again those whirling
worlds more perfectly than the room she's in,
her smile open, her glazed eyes radiant.

II

A woman who thought she loved me once wrote
a story in which "dust motes danced on and on."
It may have had a narrative, I forget.
It may have even had some characters,
men and women or domestic animals
going about their made-up lives. I remember
the story won a prize, was published, brought
her momentary attention and money
enough to take me to lunch. I hated
the way she ate, her clothed arms close to her sides,
one hand clutching a napkin with which
she feverishly dabbed at her lips as though
ingesting her chicken salad were an act
against God or some vast cosmic principle.
When I looked at my own right hand that held
a soggy golden french fry, I saw the nails
begrimed with grease, the yellow calluses
thick on my palm and cracked fingers, and felt
spectacularly pleased simply to be me,
a dirty Detroit Jew with bad manners.

III

"Without our bodies we cannot love,"
someone once wrote. On my 70th birthday
my wife asks me what I want. I do not
have long to consider. "Just you," I say.
I live now across from a funeral parlor
where even on Sunday mornings the hearses
are taken out and first hosed down for hours,
then dried carefully and polished, slick black
'88 Lincolns tailored for their jobs
so that the dead of North Carolina
can be smoothly and dustlessly chartered
to their carved earthen holes. The gnarled old man
who commands hose and chamois wears yellow boots,
his black jeans tucked inside, spits tobacco juice
while singing hoarsely. "Can you smell the pulp mill?"
he once asked when I went out to fetch the paper.
"When the wind's wrong, they tell me it's bad."
Scarlet fever had killed his sense of smell
in childhood, and he now counts himself lucky
in his line of work on these warm winter days.

IV

One late-winter afternoon, waiting alone
to see a friend, I wrote "Dust Me" with my finger
on the huge green leaf of an elephant ear
in her cozy sunroom. The little request
would remain as long as the plant remained, somehow
etched in my script. Years passed before my friend
told me how deeply her mother had been hurt
by this thoughtless act I in my merriment
thought clever. I remember Mrs. Kurian
later answering the door without a smile,
her eyes cast down, no doubt doing her best
to forgive me. She died and was mourned
by her five daughters. I remember my friend
sat by the deathbed thinking, My mother
is not here. Alone, the father hung on,
determined, though the house was looted, and he
mugged in his own driveway. A proud man, Roy,
he died in a rest home in San Jose
among strangers years after the house was sold
to a city councilman who raised pigs
illegally in spotless pens in the backyard.

V

On a TV spectacular the cosmos
spins like a snow shower in a light show
of heavenly bodies. I'm reminded of Dust Bowl
photographs in *Life* magazine: a farmer
and his woman run toward shelter while the earth
they tore some living from rises against them
with all its plenitude. The man and woman
are not driven from their garden in shame
as in a painting, their mouths broken with moans.
These two borrow a Ford with bad tires and worse spares;
they have themselves and three kids to feed, and so
like the wind they head west where perhaps the land
has settled down, decided to be merely
the land they'll someday take up living in.
Even the atom may be largely empty space,
the TV says. Einstein and Niels Bohr quarrel
for days and resolve nothing. Tonight my wife
holds a glass of black Catalan wine up
to the candlelight and drinks to my New Year
and I to hers, acts as good as any
to stall our time from whirling into dust.

III

NAMING

Do you remember an impossible city
on the river Styx, population depressed,
altitude a mile below everything?
Someone presentable had to be mayor,
someone clever had to be treasurer,
tax collector, keeper of the cooked books.
The state of Michigan in 1928,
the cracker invasion waiting in the wings.

In the endless month of that year's winter came
the wise and tiny children of the wolf,
Last Hope and First Curse disguised as boys,
even at birth brimming with the knowledge
of who they were: the eyes and ears of hell.
They would record the green leaf's bursting out,
the gray rain's song, the sparrow's rise and fall.

                    •

The seasons changed around them and they changed,
slowly growing into the names they answered to
until they thought they were those names—
soldiers and conquerors, though in the streets
just kids fighting to be kids, kids who knew
they had their special work cut out:
the crushed cat dying to be heard, the oil
along the curbs, the sun transformed in filth.

On an ordinary day late one summer
a crow attacked a hawk in plain sight
above the apartment house. That was the cue:
Time to get going! So one took on
the sparrow's conscience and sang to no one
the nothing he knew, the other found
his colors in muffled light or none at all.

•

Count on the weather. Seventy-one
years ago my father climbed the stairs
to the back porch with two bottles
of frozen milk. He stamped the snow
off his wing tips. A few stars
sparked in his hair and slowly
faded away. The cream rose through
the bottle tops. The first bite thrilled.

When my father sat down to coffee,
a cigarette, and the *Free Press*
while he hummed "Home on the Range,"
it was I who smashed my fist down
on the table. Where was oatmeal,
where was my orange? I howled for what
was mine and got laughter instead.

•

Over and over we live
that perfect winter of '33,
the ethereal music
of snow falling into snow
all night long. At dawn Yetta,
my doomed aunt, comes home
in a taxi, her eyes smeared,
her new silk hose safe, buried

in the borrowed leather purse
between her legs. Uncle Nate,
not yet my uncle, rises
at noon already knowing
the nothing he needs to know,
grunts out two dozen push-ups,
and brushes his teeth with beer.

•

Sooner or later the death angel enters
these lives or others. Let the day be bright
in early autumn, let it be morning
with sunlight streaming through broad windows
on a usual school day. Pushed to one side
of what we thought was ours, we stand for hours
wondering, Who are these people in our lives
talking in voices that were never theirs?

Soon this will end, we think, and we'll go back
to who we were. But it won't be that way.
Something is missing. Look in the closets,
or under the bed where Mama would look,
search every face. Something is still missing,
though we search the cupboards, the sofa,
all our pockets, even our memories.

•

Snow on the hooded car, the iron fence,
but no longer falling, the sky clear,
the light glorified, a new world
stretching as far as sight allows
and beyond. A hidden door opens,
a child imagines the cold rushing
into his lungs, the sudden thrill
of breath arriving and the pain.

Stumbling down the alley, a horse cart
piled with mementos of the life
to come. Eyes tight against the cold,
the child leaves for school, the skirts
of his coat scrolling his secrets
in the snow. The street crows scatter
in a cold wind from the northwest.

•

The mother back from Europe with a gift
for her quiet boy, a painted rubber ball
from Holland. The son knows
a war is coming. Already he can smell
the cities burned to ash. Here the full moon
hangs above the outdoor beer garden
where his young mother twirls in the arms
of someone he's never seen before, a man

in high dark trousers, tie, and pressed shirt.
If he closes his eyes so as not to see,
the man will still be there, closer, seated
with a glass of beer in one hand, a cigarette
in the other, and if he opens them he'll find
bare linden branches, men in long coats half-
buried in snow, their eyes frozen open.

•

The finance company drove off one night
with the blue Olds two-door and under
the door left a receipt my mother
swallowed with her morning coffee.
No, she didn't cry, not my mother.
Sweating in the greasy Persian lamb,
she cursed heaven in God's own words
and—galoshes buckled—was out the door.

Mother believed she was American.
She'd survived steerage, a volcanic father,
two husbands in junk, decades
of corporate serfdom, a love affair
with a third-rate sculptor from L.A.,
the beauty of Yiddish, the lost words
rising in her heart until her heart broke.

•

Castor and Pollux they later
read about in an illustrated
volume stolen from the local
library. Everything they read
was stolen or free. The mauve air
they breathed was free, the Milky Ways
they ate, stolen, the school lunches
with milk—chocolate or plain—were free,

the lessons in diplomacy
that didn't take, in fisticuffs
that did, in humiliation—
public and private—in patience,
revenge, class warfare, square dancing,
sexual intercourse, everything
they received was stolen or free.

•

Until he dies, a boy remains a boy.
In Michigan he can die five days a week
into a rusted brake drum, a tie rod,
a blown manifold, a three-beer breakfast,
a broth of hydrochloric acid, and once he dies
he's less than nothing, an aura wandering
between parked cars. To be alive, nameless,
still young, searching for anything, to be

outside the Avalon at 2 a.m.
when the lights blink off, the kids leave in pairs,
to be alone then, hearing only breath,
your own breath rising to answer with words
you didn't know you knew the pale questions
of the full moon, to know for the first time
you are you without a name or number.

•

Late summer of '45. My older brother
back from war. Awake, waiting for light
to flood the room when a voice cries out,
my voice in dreams. Later he and I tramp
through the empty fields at the edge of town
and into the shaded woods. I show him
a tight nest of broken eggs, a fresh hole
the field mice made, a wren's gray remains,

all the small secrets that contain me.
He doesn't ask if the cry was mine.
He says nothing about the daylight raids
on the French villages. Though it's still August
the seasons blow around us, night and cold rain
waiting in the air we breathe, two brothers
held together by what they can't share.

•

How to explain a singular genius
rising as though by magic from the great
slag hills that burned night and day outside
the family hovel? At thirteen he could name
the stars we never saw, a thousand
thousand in French or Latin or Zulu
if need be. Before he became a man
he became our imperfect Other, our myth.

Tall, slender, the classic Slavic features
puffed and blooded from alcohol or tears,
he pulled night shifts at Railway Express
all the long winter of his tragic year
with only beer for lunch. At midnight walked
back to work under a sky scored by snow
that ached like him and prayed for tenderness.

•

Clark was the guy who ran the gas station;
it said so on his shirt. From behind the desk
in the glass office he'd come out to ask
what would it be. Late May, rationing over,
you could buy all the gas you could pay for.
It was a free country for anyone
with money. From nowhere a little stray
with stained and matted fur began to run

around and around the pumps, snapping
his jaws and barking. "Yours?" Clark asked.
When I said no he kicked savagely at him,
lost his balance, and had to grab my arm.
Not yet 6:30, new sunlight filtering
through a stand of ceremonial elms
just budding out behind the used-car lots.

•

The black river at dawn, the long boats drifting
in early spring while strange flowers burst
in the oiled meadows outside Ford #7,
the sky softened without a lark's song
to the soiled world. Before the night ended
we'd crossed to Canada and headed east
toward Boston or New York, I forget which
since we never got there. A new war looming,

the first to repossess Asia—
a war someone needed. Northwest of Erie
the road ran out on us or we ran off it
to come to rest in a field of sweet corn
shivering in the winds off the planet Mars.
"Brother," you said, while you leaned in to me,
gasping with laughter, "what horse shit is this?"

•

Always there was music, Clifford and Max
one month, Miles the next, Lester Young
near the end, half sober, the high off-
center wail of the horn like a
voice heard before we heard voices.
On the Saturday singalong from the Met
in the back of D'Angelo & Ferente's
French Cleaners & Fine Alterations,

the tiny Sicilian coat maker
on tiptoe to reach the high notes
along with Björling. Della Daubien
on the crosstown streetcar as dusk
rises from the trees. If you go back
you'll hear her rough alto echoing
down the bombed-out streets of heaven.

•

The Mother of the Other, she's fixed in time
beside the brother, Walter, who escaped
to Traverse City. We celebrate him too,
the sister as well, Terese. Dearborn,
mid-century: it must be a wedding,
the witnesses are here, and the shadow
across the new husband's face is not
the shadow of anything. I know because

I took the picture with an Argus C3
my uncle got in London to photo-
graph the ruined cities along the Rhine
from his B-17. The shadow was there, asleep
in the camera on the long sea voyage
home from war, waiting patiently for
this bright appointment with the bridegroom.

•

"Good men!" Never within earshot spoken
to my ragged collection demolishing
U.S. 24, that reached all the way
to the kingdom of Toledo and beyond.
Eleven of us worked twelve-hour days
seven days a week so that the old road
would never again bear the twin weights
of commerce for many, adventure for few.

Summer of '50, of gray skies and some
higher power that brought loud night storms
to fill the shallow culverts we all the long
mornings dug, that brought old Cherry's
second stroke that stopped him for good
beside the savaged elms and honey locusts
the roadside kids marveled to see felled.

•

In the parking lot of the Grosse Pointe
Ladies' Association, four crows
circle a Chevy pickup as though
it were a rotting animal
instead of steel, plastic, rubber, glass,
whatever. Three times a week
all summer the Ukrainian gardener
waters the parking lot. It's a job.

"The desert bloomed, so just maybe
the cement," he says. "One time
I told them it cannot happen."
The beauty of such speech, of language
itself: the words catch something
incomprehensible. The senior crow
tastes a fender, then a front tire.

Naming

•

Stanzyk calls. Needs money to bail out
his crazy sister Dottie or they'll put
her six-year-old in foster care.
What she do this time? I ask. *In church
she nailed the faggot priest, a Nazi,
wouldn't accept her confession 'cause
her kid's a nigger. That's her excuse.*
Doesn't explain the sculpture torn

from a pedestal, a terra-cotta
virgin and child, smashed on the altar.
By noon Dot's free, little Hawkins home,
I'm light dollars and cents, Stanzyk's
on a bar stool at Zoisha's swapping
a version of the day's events for shots
of Stoli—Stanzyk, our fabulist, our Ovid.

•

One morning the phone rings and
you answer. It could be *Time*
requesting an interview
or the king of Spain offering
amnesty. It's Mrs. Strempek
calling from Michigan, not too
early she hopes, and then silence
and you know Bernard is dead,

our genius in a one-car
accident outside Dayton.
Close your eyes and you'll see fire,
kick a stone and underneath
you'll find dirt, utter
a sound and the sky will give
back nothing. It only takes.

•

Each spring you come back to us
in the blossoms of the pear tree,
in the lost language of the spruce
trapped in sunlight, in the cry
of the one gull circling,
you come back in the cold rain
falling all night on the tin
roofs and the dry canal beds.

Again the earth drinks all that's
left of you and asks for more.
Beginning April, I go out
to the dawn fields where last
year's yellow grass still hangs on,
and I say your names, numberless,
into the wind, and it's not enough.

•

As long as there is earth under your feet
someone must dig into it. I learned this from
Sophie Psaris, who knelt to the cold ground
each March to nurse the wild flags that dotted
the junked fields behind the garage
where rats thrived on the scraps she set out:
"They have to live too." There must be a heaven
for all stray creatures, someplace with ripe fruit

steeped in rain, fields of newly turned earth
with room for the buried dead, their bodies
swollen with desire, hulking bodies
and tiny ones that once were wrens. In the dark
Sophie opens the back gate to let the aroma
of rotting roses flood the world. In my high room
I waken to the bark of a spade on stone.

57

•

When the power failed we stood in the dark
waiting for the crash of steel falling from
the overhead cranes. I could make out
Johnson, his eyes wide, the sweat starting
from his broad forehead. We lit up on one match
as tiny lights blazed all down the line
robbing the air of anything to breathe.
Outside I knew it was April. Behind the flat

on Pingree I'd planted radishes, flags,
carrots that would rot, and all afternoon
worked the soil feeling the last cold
of winter enter my legs to grope my heart.
Long Johnson took my left hand in his
so that when the lights came back I'd know
at long last we were brothers in terror.

•

"Pretty good, and you?" it begins,
though where it goes is anywhere.
A week passes. Side by side they'll
be headed toward Paris via
Ontario in a borrowed
Olds '98 when one of them says,
"Pull over." It's past 2 a.m.,
there's nothing to pull over for.

Something amazing's always ahead,
a city like no other, and their lives
waiting. When they drown the headlights,
the whole dime store of the night sky
blares into view, so let's leave them there,
both still young, still full of pleasure
in each other and in themselves.

•

"Does the wind have a name?" Eugene asks me
from a phone booth outside the old grease shop.
(This must be a dream.) "Does the what?" I say
pretending I haven't heard. His voice fades out
as the jet fighters take off at dawn and set
my house roaring as though invaded
by an ocean. The operator breaks in to ask
if I'll accept the charges. Eugene's alone,

it's winter in Michigan with snow falling
in the twilight and hiding the stalled cars
on Grand River. Head whitened with snow,
Eugene lets the receiver slip from his hand.
I can see his eyelashes weighted with ice,
his brown eyes slowly closing on the image
of who I was, who I will always be.

IV

1/1/2000

In Joe Pryskulnik's darkened kitchen the face
of Jesus appears on a dish towel, but no one's awake
to bear witness. Next door to the fenced truck yard
behind my father's grease shop where all time stopped
there's a hive of activity. You're thinking
the rats found a wolverine or the guard dogs
caught another kid strung out on crack. You're thinking
two thousand years passed in the blink of an eye
and changed nothing, the eaters went on eating,
their crazed teeth clicking with delight. You're thinking
that's my mother rising from the ashes of her years,
her robes signed with axle grease, her hair stained
by the new dawn. It's not. It's not J.P. either,
for Joe's gone west in a box, it's not my father
come back after sixty-seven years in the wrong direction,
into the earth that gagged on motor oil, the earth
that gave back wild phlox, flags, weeds, unasked
for each April. You're thinking the dawn won't break,
that time will end because it must, and the face of Christ
will blaze in the darkness of a loveless century
while the cat and the mouse slumber side by side
in this impossible kingdom. Tomorrow is on
the way, an hour ago the sun broke through
the thatched roof of Rassan the Messenger,
scarring the silent forehead on which the ants
replayed their games. Before you can blink, the light
will blister the gray hair of Margaret Baxter
to reveal two hands swollen like potatoes and crossed
on her breast. Let Scotland mourn her loss,
let the waves off Scapa Flow work less and less
as the departed join the patient families
of the drowned. Let us honor her life with a feast
of potatoes, the million and one she scrubbed

and peeled, and garlic and onion for Andrés,
those fruits of his labor, of his one lifetime
in Haskell, New Jersey, where now he resides
in Rousek's Catholic Funeral Home without *paz,*
dolor, merced, with no one to speak his name
or sing him lullabies. Let the new day
break on the fenced yard, let it fill the kitchen
with light overflowing the stained shot glass
Joe left behind, the grail of his hopes, let it rust
with animal blood the blurred face of Jesus
on the Shroud of Michigan and westward move
across blackened Gary, the frozen prairies,
the great divide, to find us in the valleys
of our living where we surrendered our names
and natures, with all that made us human, let it
go on, this empty fraction of eternity,
to die at last in the ocean of its birth.

YENKL

He blessed each weed budding in the spring fields.
To him the mornings were music, with the rain
glistening softly on the scattered stones
all the long spring days while the sparrow hawks
circled slowly over the weed patches.

My great-uncle Yenkl had done his time,
thirty years in Siberia, felling
giant birch trees summer and winter.
After one crushed his leg he made his way
by night to Inchon and the Americans,

who sent him on to me. 1955.
The oldest stock boy in Christendom
working nights at Safeway, to pay
for his own washing machine and dryer.
His plan was simple: to join his family

in Israel. One evening after dinner
two weeks before he left he asked to pray
with me, to give thanks, he in Russian,
I in English. "Not in Hebrew?" I asked.
Only the righteous could pray in Hebrew—

God might hear and punish both of us.
Who was there for him to thank
and for what? The years in prison,
the gift of a maimed leg on which he'd take
his morning walk, listing back and forth,

no matter what the weather? So we prayed
side by side before the blank TV,
bowing and rising while my kids stared.
The appliances floated on ahead by ship
to Haifa to find his sons grown to manhood.

Today I'd walk the fields in the winter chill
if the fields were still here and not the dull miles
of suburban houses. May the rain fall
on the little graveyard where he now lies
in an unmarked grave in the Judean hills,

may it pool on the hard yellow clay
so unheard music can rise and descend,
may the earth hear and rejoice in his gifts,
the bounty of one who took what was given,
may it bless him in the language of the wind.

MY FATHER IN THE WIND

Even in the dark the wind blows. I hear it
in the high branches of the great cedar
humming its one tune. In the small room
that is mine the dust grains refuse to speak
although they know it all, for they contain
the ashes of my father, being far older
than time, and the singular pain of his father
who took his own life and left his son
no final word, only silence and an open door
through which the boy—my father—discovered
the unfamiliar humped shadow swinging
in no wind. Orphaned, the boy did not
sit down by the waters of the Dnieper to weep
as a man might do in a sacred text, he did not
curse God or howl or simply stand stunned
by the bright sun's arrival on such a day
or even beg a neighbor to cut down
the body. He climbed a ladder, braced his legs
against the top rung, and with a rusted saw
and one hand guiding the blade,
the other pulling through the golden bands
of sisal, slowly severed whatever
connected his father's body to its final act.

You might well ask how I know all this
since the dust that was there is silent still.
You think my father never spoke? You think
because he was tall, dark-suited, responsible,
and I was a kid he wouldn't turn suddenly
when the traffic stalled and address me
as he might address the wind? He would be dust.
He'd learned that twenty years before on that day
in Dobrovica in autumn, the day the wind called

to him from the plane trees flanking the river
to say, "Here's your secret!" The light attacked
through the mismatched boards of the barn roof.
Rain was on the way, but that was days off.
The golden afterthoughts of hay, fodder,
and dried horse dung rose in the air to form
a message only a fatherless child could read.
Another wind blew last night, the same wind
through the same cedars that welcomed me
back from madness thirty years ago and brought
the blessing I required. The wind can do that,
it can carry all the voices of the living
and the dead, but the dust holds its knowledge.

The dust said nothing on that morning
in 1933 when my father leaned his forehead down
on the steering wheel and spoke in Arabic
to tell me alone all he'd been and all
he would become. He loved those strange words.
He shouted the sudden plosives and the vowels
deep as moonlight and gave me each word
a second time as he took my hand in his
for the long moment until the traffic light
on Grand River turned from red to green
so we could enter the past. Since then I've misplaced
that tiny ideogram of his life etched in dust.
In its stead I have the Atlas cedar and the aspen
carrying the wind's words, the scraps
fluttering from the garbage—newspapers
stamped with no truths—a single mockingbird
rehearsing his psalms, and over the back fence
the scattered omens that rehearse the future,
a scum of graying clouds off the plating plant

garbling the constant message of the dead.

THE INVENTION OF THE FADO

"Our Miasma," the locals call it, city
of hills, old barrios, a great harbor.
The year is 1904, a war beginning
in the east. Deserters, anarchists, Jews
come for refuge. We could be among them—
though we aren't—men without women,
on fire with longing. I'll show you one,
my grandfather, Yusel Pryskulnik, who performs
in the Café Tulipe. Look how he stands,
one hand thrust into his jacket pocket,
a cotton scarf around his throat, a gray fedora
tipped slightly back, and stares into the haze
of tobacco smoke and does not even blink.
You are not this man chanting Sephardic hymns,
you did not lose an older brother, dragged
off one dawn by the police in long gray coats,
never to return, nor did you watch your father
hung for butchering a chicken on a saint's day.
He enters your life slowly, not in the song
that lingers above the drinkers, not in smoke
blown over water or salt spray or words
put down by me or even the whisper
of his own voice, raw, torn, and barely heard
above the roar of all the waiting wars.
Lisbon was his: the young—both rich and poor—
climbed the cobbled lanes of the Alfama
to wait for hours to hear the faint echo
of his private sorrows. Widows in black,
half-drunken sailors, men without mothers
wept to hear music that was not music.
One day he was gone into no one knows what,
gone forever, and the songs vanished with him.
Now, go to the mirror. Look: it's not you

as you thought you were, it's not me either,
it's not anyone we worked to become.
It's spring of 2000. The wild roses riot
along the fence, the lilacs are late
to cast their shade on the purple mounds
we bowed to, and again the dead have found
a way into the hearts we swore were stone.

WHEN THE SHIFT WAS OVER

When the shift was over he went out
and stood under the night sky a mile
from the darkened baseball stadium
and waited for the bus. He could taste
nickel under his tongue, and when he swiped
the back of his hand across his nose
he caught the smell of hydrochloric acid.
There were clouds between him and the stars,
not ordinary ones but dark and looming,
and if rain had begun to fall, he thought,
could it be black? Could a halo form
on those fine curls his Polish grandma
loved to brush when he was a boy, cupping
a hand under his chin? How silent
and still the world was after so much
slamming of metal on metal and the groans
of the earth giving way to the wakened fury
of machines and the separate cries of people
together for these nights. How odd that he,
born of convicts and soldiers, men
and women who crossed and recrossed the earth
carrying only the flag of their hopes,
should stand numbed by the weight
of a Thursday shift and raise his head
to a heaven he'd never believed in and sing
in a hoarse voice older than his years,
"Oh, Lordy Lord, I am, I'm coming home!"
He, who had no home and no hope, alone
on a certain night in a year of disbelief,
could sing to the ranks of closed houses
and cars, could sing as clear rain fell.

ON A PHOTOGRAPH OF
SIMON KARADAY

"April 12, 1938"
in my mother's cursive beneath
a picture of Simon K the day he left
for Caracas and never wrote back
as I knew he wouldn't. A raw day,
a thin trail of smoke or clouds above
us, Simon and me, as we trudged
the long blocks in silence—or so
memory and imagination
construct it. What followed I'll
never forget, the gift of
his silver ring. His finger coated
with spit, he screwed it off,
took my left hand in his, and closed it
on the ring just as the bus arrived.
That was that. I was eleven, quick
for my age and suddenly inspired
by a world I could only fantasize,
the world of the great explorers, those
who spent their final years on lost
Pacific islands and left behind
journals no one read or sullen letters
never mailed. Uncle Simon left
behind almost nothing: a radio,
a pair of black Wellingtons—the toes
turning up, the leather gone gray,
cracking—and his huge work gloves,
gauntlets he called them, sweat-stiffened,
reeking of him. And a few books:
*The Wisdom of the Body, Handbook
of Radio Lore*, a tiny leather-bound
version of *The Odyssey* in the prose
of T. E. Lawrence. In the picture,

bareheaded, he leans against
the weight of the duffel bag and looks
as huge as remembrance. A raw scar
—unexplained—darkens his right eye,
stumbles down his cheek, and vanishes.
The ring glints on his left hand
hanging open, the palm turned
away as though to hide the rivers
of embedded grease. Who was he?
I've asked myself again and again.
Was there some mystery in his coming,
the sudden tangible presence
in our lives? There's no one to ask.
Even the house is gone, burned in '67,
taking my childhood with it.
Was he more than my Uncle K, come
from Alexandria to see his cousin,
my father, only to find him gone,
dead, and to sit alone in silence
until night filled the little room
under the stairs we called the parlor?
Our home was his, the unfinished
cellar both his bedroom and workroom,
where late into the night he bent
over his invention, the tubeless radio
he never finished. I'd hear music
or unfamiliar voices rising
when I wakened in the darkness
gasping for breath. One night I stood
in robe and slippers at the head
of the stairs and called his name
in a scared voice. Laughing, he urged
me down and showed me his tools:

needle-nosed pliers, delicate files,
brass-handled screwdrivers with
tiny knurled handles, a soldering iron
that plugged in. He tried to teach me,
but I was useless. Far too big
for my hand, the ring hung for years
from a fine silver chain around my neck.
In its center I still recall a swirl
of creatures, from stage left a horseman
anodizéd in black advancing,
his lance lowered, and above all that
another swirl of black lines, initials
maybe, or clouds of angelic wrath
directed at the world. The ring stood
for him, I thought, but each time I read it
I read it differently, and each time
I learned nothing. In the photo
his coarse hair combed back reveals
the eyes naked and welcoming,
the dark skin drawn tight across
the high Slavic cheekbones if Slavic
they were, the face of an anarchist
or a Jewish saint. He was who he was.
The harder question, the one with no
answers then or now, is *who was I.*

MY GIVEN NAME

My grandmother missed the midnight train back
and walked home to our village. The day broke
over a sleeping world. The sparrows rose
one by one to wait in line to eat shit.

Thus some months later was my father born
in a year without numbers, in a house
nailed together with smoke, in a land
no one dared to name. My life is his.

I was told to worship the first book I read,
the book of waters, written in a dry year.
"Memorize it all and say it back to me,"
said the bearded servant of the bearded lord.

Instead I counted out the letters of my name,
the name I gave myself, Fishel Efroyim.
They total lucky thirteen, forward or back,
from the middle vowel to the consonants.

These are truths told with a good intent,
little secrets I want to share, like the bread
I hid from Abraham, the delicious piss
against Adam's tree in honor of our God.

THE GENIUS

When Jake gave up his job on afternoons,
who took up his magical tools so the line
would never stop? Think of the Packard sixteens,
rolling and rolling toward paradise or

Toledo without their upholstery
perfected. Think of it in human terms,
the want of a stitch, the want of a tuck,
Lonnie the foreman howling, "Where's my kike

when I need him?," the heads of the sewers
bowed before the cloth they'll puzzle over
forevermore on earth or in heaven.
Let the whole shop know, he won't arrive;

Jacob the cutter missed the streetcar
this very afternoon and no one cried out,
"We're short a passenger, the little kike
whose bad left shoulder tilts to the right."

No one noticed, not even the conductor
busy shortchanging and punching transfers,
nor the blank assembler, nor the typist,
her scalded fingers the color of cinders.

No doubt the god of Detroit looked down
or up, however such a god might look,
and found things as usual, green
the sweet rivers of home, green as raw beer

pissed out, and the air was lavender,
and the little kike with a lilt to the right
nowhere in sight. All that afternoon
the men in upholstery did as they might

and nothing got done. The angels of Detroit,
among the silent choirs of engineers,

wept to see their industry unhoused
after so many profitable years.

The answer is: no one took up the tools,
no one took up the craft. The handmade awls,
the cruel needles, scissors, knives, all he'd sewn,
vanished with him at four in the afternoon.

This has been a short chapter in the tragedy
of my country, one without beginning,
middle, or end, as Aristotle wrote
such tales require—not having lived in Detroit—

and yet among these details abides a truth
that defines the nature of events on earth,
the perfection of the life or of the work,
and has nothing to do with Uncle Jake.

CALL IT MUSIC

Some days I catch a rhythm, almost a song
in my own breath. I'm alone here
in Brooklyn, it's late morning, the sky
above the St. George Hotel is clear, clear
for New York, that is. The radio is playing
Bird Flight, Parker in his California
tragic voice fifty years ago, his faltering
"Lover Man" just before he crashed into chaos.
I would guess that outside the recording studio
in Burbank the sun was high above the jacarandas,
it was late March, the worst of yesterday's rain
had come and gone, the sky was washed. Bird
could have seen for miles if he'd looked, but what
he saw was so foreign he clenched his eyes,
shook his head, and barked like a dog—just once—
and then Howard McGhee took his arm and assured him
he'd be OK. I know this because Howard told me
years later, told me he thought Bird could
lie down in the hotel room they shared, sleep
for an hour or more, and waken as himself.
The perfect sunlight angles into my little room
above Willow Street. I listen to my breath
come and go and try to catch its curious taste,
part milk, part iron, part blood, as it passes
from me into the world. This is not me,
this is automatic, this entering and exiting,
my body's essential occupation without which
I am a thing. The whole process has a name,
a word I don't know, an elegant word not
in English or Yiddish or Spanish, a word
that means nothing to me. Howard truly believed
what he said that day when he steered
Parker into a cab and drove the silent miles

beside him while the bright world
unfurled around them: filling stations, stands
of fruits and vegetables, a kiosk selling trinkets
from Mexico and the Philippines. It was all
so actual and Western, it was a new creation
coming into being, like the music of Charlie Parker
someone later called "glad," though that day
I would have said silent, "the silent music
of Charlie Parker." Howard said nothing.
He paid the driver and helped Bird up two flights
to their room, got his boots off, and went out
to let him sleep as the afternoon entered
the history of darkness. I'm not judging
Howard, he did better than I could have
now or then. Then I was nineteen, working
on the loading docks at Railway Express,
coming day by day into the damaged body
of a man while I sang into the filthy air
the Yiddish drinking songs my Zadie taught me
before his breath failed. Now Howard is gone,
eleven long years gone, the sweet voice silenced.
"The subtle bridge between Eldridge and Navarro,"
they later wrote, all that rising passion
a footnote to others. I remember in '85
walking the halls of Cass Tech, the high school
where he taught after his performing days,
when suddenly he took my left hand in his
two hands to tell me it all worked out
for the best. Maybe he'd gotten religion,
maybe he knew how little time was left,
maybe that day he was just worn down
by my questions about Parker. To him Bird
was truly Charlie Parker, a man, a silent note

going out forever on the breath of genius
which now I hear soaring above my own breath
as this bright morning fades into afternoon.
Music, I'll call it music. It's what we need
as the sun staggers behind the low gray clouds
blowing relentlessly in from that nameless ocean,
the calm and endless one I've still to cross.

NOTES

PAGE 10 "On 52nd Street"
The Bud of the poem is Bud Powell, the great bebop pianist. The last line owes much to the title of Thelonious Monk's composition "In Walked Bud."

PAGE 23 "My Brother, Antonio, the Baker"
The lines Antonio recites in the poem are a theft or parody of the work of the great Spanish poet Antonio Machado, whose writing abounds with references to Soria, where he lived as a young man, and the river Duero.

PAGE 36 "Breakfasts with Joachim"
Antonio Machado is often referred to as "the good Machado," to distinguish him from his poet brother Manuel, something of a dandy and a much inferior poet.

PAGE 43 "Dust" (section V)
In Spain strong red wine is often referred to as black *(negro)*.

PAGE 52 "Naming" (section 11)
In order to disguise the location of the D-day invasion of France, the Allies bombed a number of French cities and towns west of the eventual site, with terrible consequences for the local populations.

PAGE 54 "Naming" (section 15)
Clifford is Clifford Brown, the great young jazz trumpeter of the bebop years; Max is Max Roach, the great drummer Brown teamed with to head an outstanding quintet.

PAGE 63 "1/1/2000"
In 1999 I was asked to write the first fourteen lines of what was planned to be "The Millennium Poem," to be added to by a number of British and American poets and finally to be completed by me. The poem was to be placed on the Web site of Amazon.com, and the first portions did appear there; but naturally, the project floundered. Sometime

later, I decided to complete the poem using my first fourteen lines as the start; I also borrowed a number of details and one name from a section written by the Scotch poet Jackie Kay. My thanks to Kerry Fried, who invented the project, and also, of course, to Ms. Kay.

PAGE 78 "Call It Music"
Bird Flight is the name of the radio program hosted by the jazz maven Phil Schaap five mornings a week on station WKCR-FM from Columbia University. The program features the music of Charlie Parker and the other great jazz artists of that era. Howard McGhee was an outstanding jazz trumpeter during the late forties, described by *The All Music Guide to Jazz* as the "missing link" between Roy Eldridge and Fats Navarro. In the summer of 1946, during a recording session with McGhee in Los Angeles, Parker suffered a breakdown, the music of which is captured on a now famous (and for some infamous) recording of "Lover Man."

The "someone" who called the music of Charlie Parker "glad" was Larry Levis in his poem "Whitman." In the poem, Whitman comes back to life "in the glad music of Charlie Parker."

A NOTE ON THE TYPE

The text of this book was set in a typeface called Méridien, a classic roman designed by Adrian Frutiger for the French type foundry Deberny et Peignot in 1957. Adrian Frutiger was born in Interlaken, Switzerland, in 1928 and studied type design there and at the Kunstgewerbeschule in Zurich. In 1953 he moved to Paris, where he joined Deberny et Peignot as a member of the design staff. Méridien, as well as his other typeface of world renown, Univers, was created for the Lumitype photoset machine.

Composed by Creative Graphics,
Allentown, Pennsylvania

Printed and bound by
United Book Press,
Baltimore, Maryland

Designed by Iris Weinstein